CREATING Keepsakes

EDITOR-IN-CHIEF Tracy White
SPECIAL PROJECTS EDITOR Leslie Miller
ASSISTANT EDITOR Britney Mellen
SENIOR WRITER Denise Pauley
COPY EDITOR Kim Sandoval, Brittany Beattie
EDITORIAL ASSISTANTS Joannie McBride, Fred Brewer
ART DIRECTOR Brian Tippetts
DESIGNER Celeste Rockwood-Jones
PRODUCTION DESIGNERS Just Scan Me!
PRODUCTION MANAGER Gary Whitehead
FOUNDING EDITOR Lisa Bearnson
CO-FOUNDER Don Lambson

PRIMEDIA

VICE PRESIDENT, GROUP PUBLISHER David O'Neil
CIRCULATION MARKETING DIRECTORS Dena Spar, Janice Martin
PROMOTIONS DIRECTOR Dana Smith

PRIMEDIA, Inc.
CHAIRMAN Dean Nelson
PRESIDENT AND CEO Kelly Conlin
VICE-CHAIRMAN Beverly C. Chell

PRIMEDIA Enthusiast Media
EVP, CONSUMER MARKETING/CIRCULATION Steve Aster
SVP, CHIEF FINANCIAL OFFICER Kevin Neary
SVP, MFG., PRODUCTION AND DISTRIBUTION Kevin Mullan
SVP, CHIEF INFORMATION OFFICER Debra C. Robinson
VP, CONSUMER MARKETING Bobbi Gutman
VP, MANUFACTURING Gregory A. Catsaros
VP, SINGLE COPY SALES Thomas L. Fogarty
VP, MANUFACTURING BUDGETS AND OPERATIONS Lilia Golia
VP, HUMAN RESOURCES Kathleen P. Malinowski
VP, BUSINESS DEVELOPMENT Albert Messina
VP, DATABASE /E-COMMERCE Suti Prakash

PRIMEDIA Outdoor Recreation and Enthusiast Group
PRESIDENT Scott Wagner
VP, GROUP CFO Henry Donahue
VP, MARKETING AND INTERNET OPERATIONS Dave Evans

ISBN 1-929180-72-1

borders

TABLE OF
contents

>

> >

borders

In life, being shoved to the side is rarely a good thing (unless you're running with the bulls in Pamplona). It often means you've been passed over, forgotten or considered unimportant. But on layouts, what's "on the side" is quite often a border...and that's never a bad thing.

Borders are perfect for taking up space—decoratively, of course. But. they can do much more than that. They're the perfect element to catch your viewer's eye with a splash of color, texture or detail. They're the ideal canvas for testing new techniques, skillfully gathering smaller elements or including supplementary journaling in a clever way.

If you've been shoving your borders so far to the side lately that they're no longer even on your page, the ideas, techniques and trends in this book may encourage you to bring them back.

KISS KISS *kiss *KISS

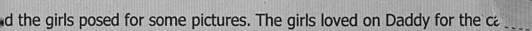
...d the girls posed for some pictures. The girls loved on Daddy for the ca...

(5)

traditional
with a twist

Nearly all scrappers have designed their fair share of "old school" borders—cardstock strips embellished with stickers, punches, die cuts and pieces of patterned paper. And while they're perfect for adding a dash of decoration to any layout, you might be in the mood to revamp your borders and create some updated looks.

This chapter will show you that it only takes a bit of added effort in the way of sanding, stitching, cutting or coloring to breathe new life into old border techniques. Combine paper, premade borders, stickers or punch outs with one of these ideas, and you'll see how easy it is to go from classic to ultracool.

GOOD TIMES: by Jamie Waters
Supplies *Patterned paper:* Making Memories (dot) and Wordsworth (pink); *Leather flowers:* Making Memories; *Letter stickers:* Wordsworth; *Pearl buckle and clay phrase:* Li'l Davis Designs; *Punch:* Marvy Uchida.

idea to note: Devise multilayered borders by using punches to create openings that can become windows for small accents.

remember GOOD times

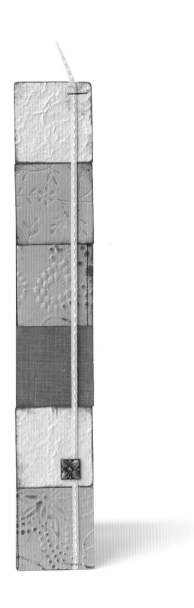

PATCHWORK: by Shannon Wolz
Supplies *Specialty papers:* Jennifer Collection (dark purple) and Memory Lane (green); *Punch:* Family Treasures; *Ribbon and brad:* Making Memories; *Stamping ink:* Ranger Industries.

idea to note: Textured paper can add instant interest to borders created from something as simple as squares. Use a bit of ribbon for even more dimension.

QUILT: by Mellette Berezoski
Supplies *Patterned papers:* Close To My Heart (green gingham), Carolee's Creations (green swirl), Mustard Moon (lime green), Daisy D's Paper Co. (multicolored stripe) and K & Company (rust gingham); *Buttons:* Junkitz.

idea to note: For a quilted effect, trim patterned paper scraps to one-inch squares and position them randomly before adhering buttons.

HAPPILY EVER AFTER: by Joy Uzarraga
Photo by Cherie Wayne. Supplies *Die cuts:* Treehouse Designs; *Gold leaf flakes:* Mona Lisa Products, Houston Art, Inc.; *Woven label:* Making Memories.

idea to note: To add glitz to preprinted die cuts, adhere gold leaf flakes to portions using liquid glue as an adhesive. *(Note:* Allow glue to dry until tacky before adhering the leaf flakes, then use a paintbrush to remove the excess.)

BIRTHDAY WISHES: by Kelly Anderson
Supplies *Die cuts:* Deluxe Cuts, Deluxe Designs; *Stickers:* me & my BIG ideas (flower) and Memories Complete (belt); *Flower accents:* SEI; *Other:* Mesh and recycled greeting cards.

idea to note: Give preprinted die cuts an added punch with stickers and cutouts from old greeting cards.

PLAY: by Miley Johnson
Supplies *Patterned paper and vellum:* KI Memories; *Solid vellum:* Autumn Leaves; *Wood letters:* Li'l Davis Designs; *Conchos:* Scrapworks; *Ribbon:* C.M. Offray & Son.

 Use vellum to create loops and tabs along your border. It can also provide a graphic look when layered over patterned paper.

LET IT SNOW: by Nichol Magouirk
Supplies *Patterned paper:* 7gypsies; *Photo border:* Shotz, Creative Imaginations; *Epoxy letter stickers:* Sonnets, Creative Imaginations; *Glass beads:* JudiKins; *Trim:* Impress Rubber Stamps; *Adhesive:* Tacky Tape, Art Accentz and Therm O Web.

idea to note: Turn premade photo borders into beaded ccents. Trim to desired size, coat with double-sided tape, dust with silver micro beads and then cover completely with clear micro beads.

GIRLIE GIRLS: by Jamie Waters
Supplies *Patterned paper and letter stickers:* KI Memories; *Stickers:* Stickopotamus; *Buckles:* Li'l Davis Designs; *Other:* Ribbon.

how to add more detail to border stickers:

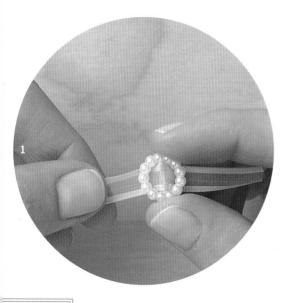

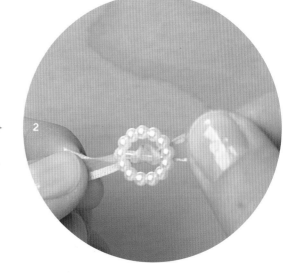

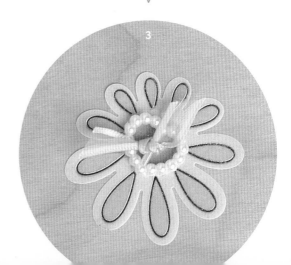

STEP 1: Thread pearl buckle with ribbon.

STEP 2: Tie knot and place glue dots on the back to secure.

STEP 3: Attach to sticker.

a case for borders

When designing a layout, the border is often the first element to be eliminated. After all, once the photos and journaling are included, there's little room left for a space-hogging border. But, you might reconsider once you realize they can be practical as well as pretty. Use borders to:

reinforce the theme of your layout. Creating a border with a design, colors, text or accents that reflect the photos can help tie all of your page elements together.

gather small items. Cluster tiny accents, photos, memorabilia and more along a border—containing them to one area will provide greater visual impact.

frame a layout. Use thin borders to surround your page and give it a finished look. Try stitched cardstock, lengths of ribbon or a string of text, for example.

cover seams. If you'd like to print a title directly onto your background but you don't have a printer large enough, simply trim a strip from the cardstock, output the text upon it, piece the background back together and use a decorative border to cover the split.

PUMPKINS: by Brenda Arnall
Supplies *Stickers:* me & my BIG ideas; *Rub-ons, eyelets and ribbon:* Making Memories; *Acrylic paint:* Liquitex.

idea to note: Resurface border stickers to give them a distressed look. Lightly sand, then apply a wash of white acrylic paint.

LEAVES: by Joy Uzarraga
Supplies *Netting:* Magic Scraps; *Punches:* Emagination Crafts; *Stamping ink:* Fluid Chalk, Clearsnap; *Staples:* Making Memories.

idea to note: Utilize punches to make quick shapes for borders. Ink the edges for a slightly shabby touch.

INSPIRE: by Jamie Waters
Supplies *Border sticker:* Pebbles Inc.; *Wood frame:* Li'l Davis Designs; *Ribbon:* Making Memories.

idea to note: Traditional border stickers receive extra dimension with the addition of smaller accents and ribbon.

SWIM: by Denise Pauley
Supplies *Patterned paper, stickers and letter stickers:* Arctic Frog.

idea to note: Large stickers don't have to be used "as is." Cut them into smaller pieces to trail along border strips.

TOGETHERNESS: by Mellette Berezoski
Supplies *Patterned paper:* Carolee's Creations; *Flower die cuts:* Paper House Productions and Remember When; *Definition sticker:* Pebbles Inc.; *Metal word plate:* Scrap Essentials, Jo-Ann Crafts; *Ribbon:* C.M. Offray & Son.

idea to note: Create height differences by adhering only one of the die cuts adorning your border with foam squares.

BABY: by Tracy Miller
Supplies *Patterned paper and punch outs:* Scrapworks; *Jump rings:* Junkitz; *Ribbon:* Li'l Davis Designs.

idea to note For a "window" effect, use a craft knife to cut "X"s into cardstock, then layer the strip over patterned paper, allowing the design to show through.

BASKETWEAVE: by Mellette Berezoski
Supplies *Patterned paper and vellum:* Chatterbox; *Brads:* Making Memories; *Circular clip:* Jest Charming.

how to weave a patterned paper border:

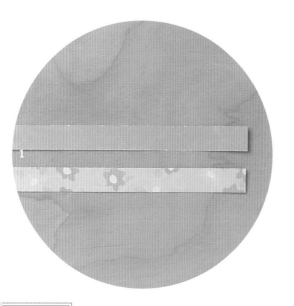

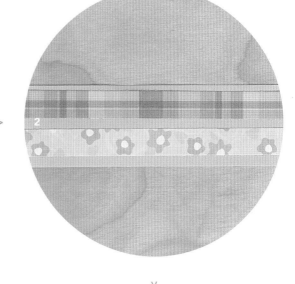

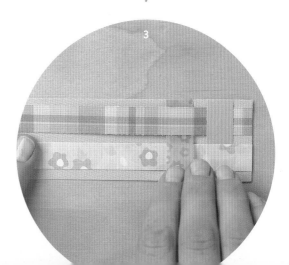

STEP 1: Cut two long strips of coordinating patterned paper.

STEP 2: Attach the two long strips to cardstock base.

STEP 3: Weave alternating short strips of vellum and patterned paper into the long strips.

SUMMER: by Jamie Waters
Supplies *Patterned paper:* American Crafts; *Circle cutter:* Creative Memories.

idea to note: Patterned paper and a circle cutter can help you make quick, cool, geometric patterns for your borders.

RED, WHITE, BLUE: by Tracy Miller
Supplies *Transparency:* Karen Foster Design; *Photo border:* Shotz, Creative Imaginations; *Photo corners:* Pioneer Photo Albums; *Pop dots:* All Night Media, Plaid Enterprises; *Label tape:* Dymo.

idea to note: To add dimension, cut a square out of the photo border and mount a transparency on it with clear photo corners. Matt the piece with black cardstock before mounting it in the original spot with pop dots.

the
perfect
friendship

These girls are
peas in a pod.

PERFECT FRIENDSHIP: by Jamie Waters
Supplies *Border stickers:* Magenta; *Rub-ons:* Making Memories; *Wood flowers:* Li'l Davis Designs.

idea to note: Border stickers aren't what they used to be—many feature cool colors, designs and hand-drawn looks to suit layouts from cute to classic.

on the border

Who says borders have to be flat and static? With a string of tags here or a dangling charm there, the edge of your page can become an attention grabber that furthers your theme and still manages to keep the focus on your photos.

Movement and dimension are yours when you choose to use a border as a collection point for small accents, photos and more. You'll be inspired by the many ways items can be attached—everything from conchos and clips to stitches and scraps can be used as decorative fasteners. Check out this chapter's projects to discover more methods to add and affix odds and ends to your borders.

FAMILY: by Joy Uzarraga
Supplies *Patterned paper:* Mustard Moon; *Frames:* Scrapworks.

idea to note: Concho-type mini frames are quick and easy to attach. Use a push pad to punch them cleanly through your cardstock. Allow them to enclose text, small photos or other accents.

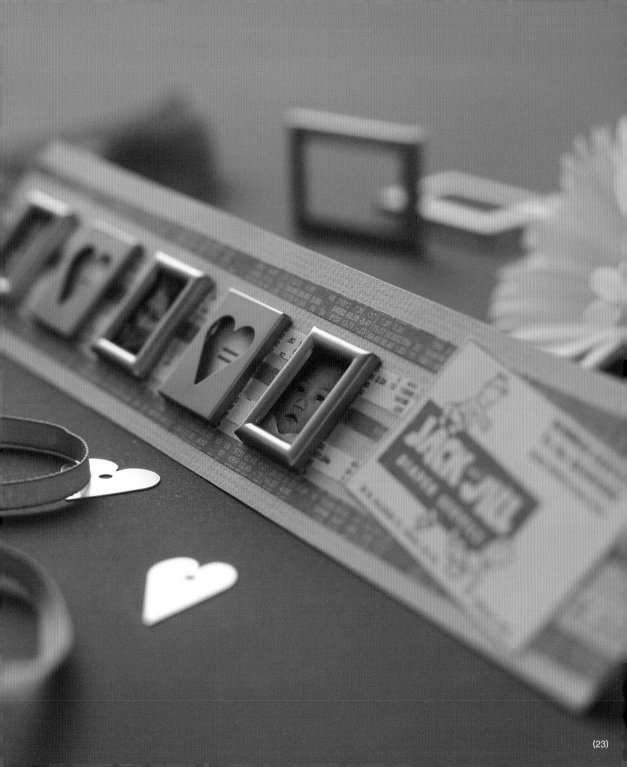

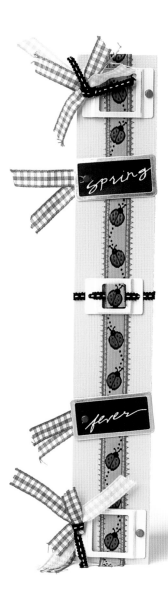

RETRO: by Denise Pauley
Supplies *Cardstock:* WorldWin; *Shapes:* Denise's own design.

idea to note: Machine stitching is a quick way to affix free-hand shapes, punches, fabric strips, die cuts and more to borders.

SPRING FEVER: by Miley Johnson
Supplies *Label holders and rub-ons:* Making Memories; *Ribbon:* C.M. Offray & Son (ladybug), Close To My Heart (gingham) and Memory Lane (black stitched).

idea to note: Label holders can be used to highlight images along your border. For a soft touch, thread and knot ribbon through the holes of label holders in place of fasteners.

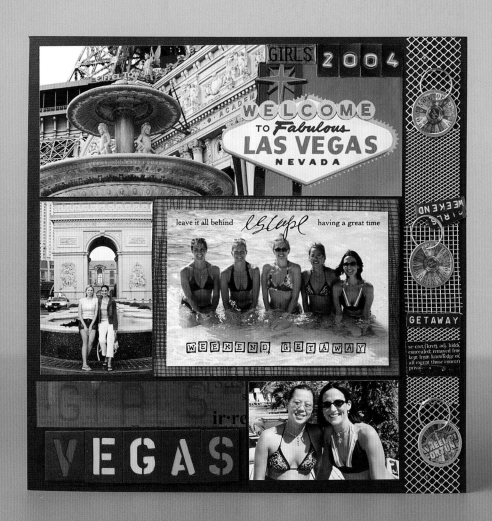

WEEKEND IN VEGAS: by Kelly Anderson
Supplies *Patterned paper:* Scrapworks; *Transparency:* Creative Imaginations; *Mesh and rub-ons:* Making Memories; *Stencil letters:* Autumn Leaves; *Pin:* Li'l Davis Designs; *Stickers:* Pebbles Inc.; *Tags:* Avery; *Labels:* Dymo; *Other:* Travel ephemera.

idea to note: Mesh is a funky border background – add to the interest by hanging items from the openings.

FLOWERS: by Nichol Magouirk
Supplies *Ribbon:* Making Memories (light purple gingham), SEI (purple silk, purple-green, purple polka dot, purple iridescent), Magic Scraps (purple gingham organza) and C.M. Offray & Son (dark purple gingham); *Buttons:* Magic Scraps; *Other:* Corduroy fabric and thread.

how to hand-sew flowers:

STEP 1: Make a small hole in the middle of the fabric. Thread ribbon through the hole with a large sewing needle.

STEP 2: Pin a second needle over the ribbon where you want the petal to end (where the fabric will fold to create the petal).

STEP 3: Insert the first needle back in the center, slightly off of the mark you entered from, completing the loop of the petal.

STEP 4: Repeat steps 1-3 for remaining petals. After completing 4 petals, remove pins and sew a button to the center of the flower.

GIGGLE: by Nichol Magouirk
Supplies *Patterned paper:* KI Memories; *Metal flowers, tags, floss and paint:* Making Memories; *Netting:* Magic Scraps; *Ribbon:* Impress Rubber Stamps (orange gingham) and SEI (green); *Other:* Charms.

idea to note: To help charms stand out against the border background, paint with various shades of acrylics before attaching to netting.

EXPERIMENT: by Tracy Miller
Supplies *Patterned paper and quote sticker:* Wordsworth; *Precut cardstock, washers and brads:* Making Memories; *Beaded chain:* Li'l Davis Designs.

idea to note: Create a quick border by trimming a strip from cardstock with precut "holes" to allow accents to show through. Use a beaded chain to add word washers to each edge.

BE YOURSELF: by Brenda Arnall
Supplies *Canvas words and pocket:* Li'l Davis Designs; *Watercolors:* Lyra; *Jump rings:* Making Memories; *Other:* Jute.

idea to note: Add a touch of color to canvas items with a wash of watercolors. Hang a small pocket on your border that can hold a personal note.

RCJ: by Joy Uzarraga
Supplies *Computer font:* Gill Sans, Monotype Corporation; *Clips:* Scrapworks; *Ribbon:* Making Memories.

idea to note: To print text behind a clip, use Microsoft Word to insert a text box into the document. Type your text and change the text color to white. Then, change the fill of the box to black.

All life is an experiment. The more experiments you make, the better.

EMERSON

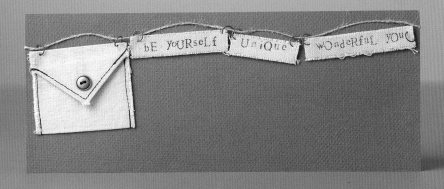

bE yOURseLf UniQue wOndeRfuL yOu

photo-inspired ideas

Borders don't always have to be pretty generic patterns or geometric designs. Incorporating elements from your photos is a great way to create harmony and support the page theme. Gather your pictures and search for ideas to replicate or play off of when creating border accents. Focus on these details:

your subject's clothing. Does she have a gorgeous hem on her dress? Is he wearing a shirt with a particularly noticeable collar? Do those often-worn shoes have a cool tread pattern?

the background. Is your subject sitting on a chair with an interesting back? Leaning against a post with a touchable texture? Standing in front of a unique fence, brick wall or sign? Look further back and take in the background...is there a section of the sky, trees, rocks or building that you can duplicate?

the occasion. Is there a perfect embellishment that represents this particular event? A color that would suit the mood? A song lyric or sentiment that suits this season?

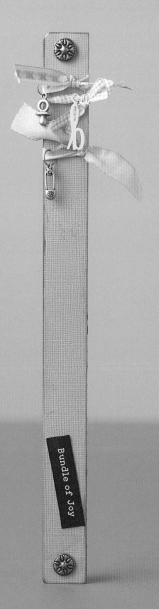

BUNDLE OF JOY: by Shannon Wolz
Supplies *Tags:* me & my BIG ideas; *Ribbon:* Impress Rubber Stamps
(green); *Alphabet charms and brads:* Making Memories; *Stamping ink:*
ColorToolBox, Clearsnap, and Hero Arts.

idea to note: For a delicate and decidedly feminine look, attach
several charms to a border strip using short lengths of ribbon.

BASEBALL: by Miley Johnson
Supplies *Patterned Paper:* Paper House Productions; *Stickers:* Karen
Foster Design; *Washers, straight pins, mesh and safety pins:* Making
Memories; *Charm:* Hobby Lobby; *Ribbon:* C.M. Offray & Son; *Other:* Twine.

idea to note: Cut holes in wire mesh to expose stickers and other
memorabilia. Attach washers to the border using long, straight pins.

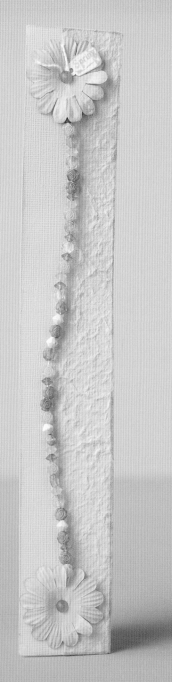

FLOWERS: by Shannon Wolz
Supplies *Flowers:* Making Memories; *Beads:* Close To My Heart; *Fasteners:* Chatterbox; *Thread:* Coats & Clark; *Other:* Wire and tag.

how to create a custom-beaded border:

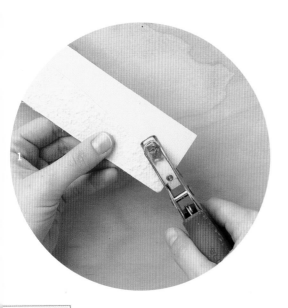

>

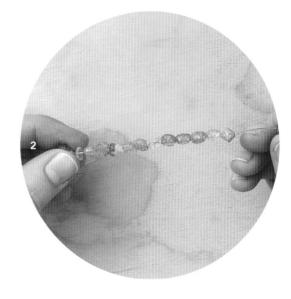

v

STEP 1: Make a border strip with two pieces of paper. Punch a small hole at each end with a hole punch.

STEP 2: String beads on a wire and attach wire to the paper strip through the holes.

STEP 3: With clear thread, sew wire to cardstock base every inch or so. Embellish as desired.

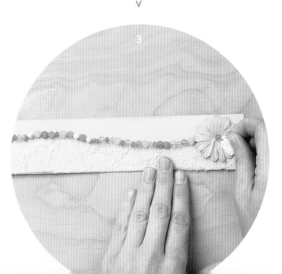

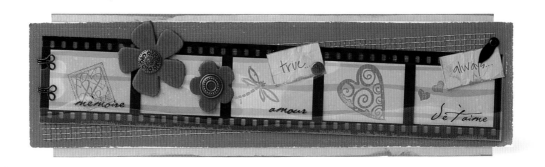

TRUE…ALWAYS…: by Denise Pauley
Supplies *Patterned paper:* The Paper Garden; *Mesh:* Sonnets,
Creative Imaginations; *Negative sleeve:* Narratives, Creative
Imaginations; *Flowers, brads, photo turn and snap:* Making
Memories; *Stamps:* Hero Arts (postage and swirl heart) and PSX
Design (dragonfly and small hearts); *Stamping ink:* VersaMagic,
Tsukineko; *Pen:* Zig Millennium, EK Success.

idea to note: Fasteners of all types make quick work of
border attachments…try using brads, eyelets, photo turns, sewing
notions and more.

DANCE: by Kelly Anderson
Supplies *Metal letters:* Making Memories; *Spiral clips:* Clipiola; *Pen:*
Zig Millennium, EK Success.

idea to note: Spiral clips can adorn border strips and be called
upon to hang other decorative items, such as metal letters.

GIDDY UP: by Miley Johnson

Supplies *Patterned paper and leather paper:* K & Company; *Computer font:* CK Corral, "Fresh Fonts" CD, *Creating Keepsakes; Alphabet stamps:* PSX Design; *Letter die cuts:* QuickKutz; *Metal letters and tag:* Making Memories; *Brads:* Lasting Impressions for Paper; *Other:* Fabric and buckle.

idea to note: Use fabric strips to attach buckles to your border for a boyish, western look.

FLOWERS: by Brenda Arnall
Supplies *Rubber stamps:* Hero Arts; *Watercolors:* Lyra; *Safety pins:* Making Memories; *Ribbon:* Making Memories (pink gingham) and C.M. Offray & Son (solid pink).

idea to note: String tags together with small pins for a dainty border. To further soften the images, color your stamps with watercolors.

BABY LOVE: by Tracy Miller
Supplies *Patterned paper, punchout words and studs:* Scrapworks; *Rubber stamps:* Wordsworth; *Stamping ink:* Nick Bantock, Ranger Industries.

idea to note: Use multicolored cardstock strips and studs to attach accents such as cardstock punch outs to your border.

GINA: by Mellette Berezoski
Supplies *Patterned paper:* Daisy D's Paper Co. (plaid) and Carolee's Creations (writing tablet); *Cork:* RoseArt; *Alphabet stickers:* me & my BIG ideas (wood grain), Creative Imaginations (black), The Paper Loft (green) and The Scrapbook Wizard (pink); *Vellum flowers:* Jolee's Boutique, Sticko for EK Success; *Word stickers and tag:* Making Memories; *Jewel brads:* Magic Scraps.

idea to note: A mini corkboard is a clever way to convey your subject's personality.

bits and pieces

Whoever said it's the little things that matter may have been onto something. While we're often "wowed" by bigger and better, we study and remember the particulars—the intricacies that keep us interested and engaged.

Though borders may be large elements, consider creating them from or enhancing them with smaller embellishments. Whether they're clustered, sewn, strung or stuck, little trimmings—from tiles to tokens and zippers to flowers—can give borders a big dose of eye-catching detail. Use the subsequent projects for a bit of inspiration—you'll discover that just because accents are undersized, that doesn't mean that they'll be overlooked.

SWEET AND SASSY: by Nichol Magouirk
Supplies *Patterned papers and letter stickers:* Sonnets, Creative Imaginations and SEI; *Transparency:* Art Warehouse, Creative Imaginations; *Paper flowers:* Savvy Stamps; *Zipper:* Junkitz; *Tag:* Avery; *Walnut ink:* Anima Designs; *Jump rings:* Making Memories; *Other:* Lace.

idea to note: Attach the zipper, leaving it halfway open so the transparency strip behind it peeks out from the opening.

ALMOST FOUR: by Shannon Wolz
Supplies *Patterned paper, vellum and acrylic accents:* KI Memories; *Brads:* Karen Foster Design; *Alphabet stamps, date stamp and sticker:* Making Memories; *Stamping ink:* Ranger Industries; *Other:* Twill and chipboard.

idea to note: Borders don't always have to be constructed from paper...arrange a slew of small photos along the edge of your page instead.

ALL GIRL: by Joy Uzarraga
Supplies *Patterned paper:* Paperfever; *Letter stickers:* Déjà Views, The C-Thru Ruler Co.; *Tags:* Avery; *Ribbon:* Bucilla, CM Offray & Son, Making Memories and May Arts; *Rickrack:* Wrights; *Stamping ink:* ColorToolBox, Clearsnap, and Dauber Duos, Tsukineko.

idea to note: Use stamping ink to customize plain white tags to match your patterned paper.

BUTTONS: by Kelly Anderson
Supplies *Conchos:* Scrapworks; *Other:* Buttons.

idea to note: Buttons, conchos, typewriter keys and round acrylic tiles give borders a whimsical and slightly geometric look.

more border brainstorming

Borders are all around us—all you have to do is look. Study the top, bottom or sides of almost any object, and you're likely to find something fascinating. It may be a pattern, a texture or a decoratively finished edge. You might also consider these elements:

walls. Check out crown moldings, baseboards, curtains, blinds, wallpaper borders and stenciling.

flooring. Note the perimeter of area rugs, stepping stones, brickwork, tile designs and grouting.

linens. Take a look at the edges of towels, blanket banding, pillowcases and dust ruffles.

clothing. Notice hemlines, necklines, belts and edgings on pants and cuffs.

internet ads. Look at the ways bands of color, text, patterns and small photos have been incorporated along the side.

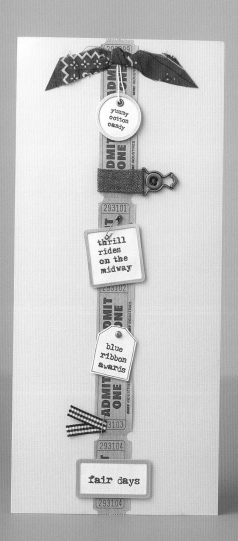

FAIR DAYS: by Brenda Arnall
Supplies *Patterned paper:* Chatterbox; *Computer font:* GF Halda, downloaded from the Internet; *Tags, brad, eyelet, pin and ribbon:* Making Memories; *Pen:* Zig Millennium, EK Success; *Suspender:* JHB International; *Other:* Tickets, fabric and string.

idea to note: A string of tickets is an imaginative border backdrop for fair, carnival and amusement park pages.

RELATIONSHIPS: by Jamie Waters
Supplies *Patterned paper, frames and concho:* Scrapworks; *Stickers:* Cloud 9 Design (quote) and Pebbles Inc. (envelope); *Rub-ons:* Li'l Davis Designs; *Other:* Ribbon.

idea to note: Small frames can turn your border into a gorgeous mini photo display.

SPRING: by Brenda Arnall

Supplies *Patterned papers:* KI Memories (background) and Colors By Design (plaid); *Pen:* Zig Millennium, EK Success; *Rub-ons and flowers:* Making Memories; *Watercolors:* Lyra; *Flowers:* Making Memories; *Brads:* Lasting Impressions for Paper; *Other:* Fiber and string.

idea to note: Apply watercolors to plain string to help it match your layout's color scheme.

HOW OLD?: by Tracy Miller
Supplies *Patterned paper and paint swatches:* Daisy D's Paper Co.; *Quote sticker:* Wordsworth; *Ribbon:* Making Memories; *Conchos:* Scrapworks.

idea to note: Cut up paint swatches for a colorful addition to borders.

FLOWERS: by Tracy Miller
Supplies *Patterned paper and Wax floss:* Scrapworks; *Wood flowers:* Li'l Davis Designs; *Charms:* Hirschberg Schutz & Co.

idea to note: Alternate charms and small wood shapes along your border for a delicate floral look.

POSTCARDS: by Kelly Anderson
Supplies *Patterned paper:* Pebbles Inc.; *Other:* Mini postcards.

idea to note: An assortment of mini postcards and vintage letters form the perfect border for travel or heritage pages.

FESTIVE: by Miley Johnson
Supplies *Metal strips:* Making Memories; *Brads:* Lasting Impressions for Paper; *Other:* Fabric.

how to create a fabric fringe border:

>

STEP 1: Cut fabric into small blocks. To fray edges, simply pull loose threads along each side.

v

STEP 2: Adhere pieces of fabric onto cardstock base or machine stitch.

STEP 3: Layer metal strip and knotted fabric strip over original piece and embellish as desired.

SMILE: by Denise Pauley
Supplies *Patterned paper:* Making Memories (pink) and KI Memories (yellow); *Fabric:* Junkitz; *Tokens:* Dot Talk, Creative Imaginations (big circles) and Doodlebug Design (small squares); *Wax floss:* Scrapworks; *Ribbon:* Making Memories (yellow) and C.M. Offray & Son (blue).

idea to note: An array of vibrant acrylic tokens adds a funky touch to borders for teen pages.

CARNIVAL: by Kelly Anderson
Supplies *Patterned paper:* Scrapworks; *Stickers:* Karen Foster Design.

idea to note: Designing pages about county fairs, city festivals or school carnivals? Use a line of tickets to create an appropriately fun and bright border.

SUMMER OF 2003: by Nichol Magouirk

Supplies *Patterned paper, label, die cuts and acrylic flowers:* KI Memories; *Label stickers, puzzle pieces and rub-ons:* Li'l Davis Designs; *Transparency and stickers:* Art Warehouse, Creative Imaginations; *Staples and stickers:* Making Memories; *Stamping ink:* ColorToolBox, Clearsnap; *Other:* Ribbon.

idea to note: Borders can also double as title blocks! To customize white alphabet puzzle pieces, press ink pads directly onto each piece. Hasten the drying process with a heat gun.

WINTER: by Tracy Miller
Supplies *Rub-on words and tin tiles:* Making Memories; *Snowflake stickers:* Tumblebeasts Stickers; *Alphabet stamps:* PSX Design; *Stamping ink:* StazOn, Tsukineko.

how to create "printed" tin tiles:

STEP 1: Peel an edge of texture sticker from the sticker backing and adhere tin tile underneath.

STEP 2: Trim the sticker to the edge of the tin tile.

v

a creative streak

It's always magical to make something out of nothing—to start with a blank slate and fashion something beautiful, artistic and cool. To design borders that are not only a reflection of your page theme but also an expression of your creative side, experiment with mediums and coloring tools.

Use products such as Ultra Thick Embossing Enamel, modeling paste or watercolors to generate borders straight from your own imagination. Or, if you'd rather, begin with a premade border and use mediums to add some attention-grabbing dimension or to develop a bit of touchable texture. Read on to discover ways to build artistic borders that are always uniquely you.

ESCAPE: by Jamie Waters
Supplies *Vellum and tab:* KI Memories; *Rubber stamps:* Close To My Heart; *Sticker:* Pebbles, Inc.; *Rub-ons and staple:* Making Memories; *Bleach pen:* The Clorox Company.

idea to note: Use a bleach pen to draw a funky custom background pattern onto cardstock. Top it off with a strip of striped vellum and a colorful tab for a cool look.

exploring the

CORNISH
coast

Bays, cliffs and granite; our travels to the towns of Cornwall:
St. Mawes
Cadgwith
Lizard Point
Penzance
Newlyn
Mousehole
Lands End
St. Just
St. Ives

CORNISH: by Brenda Arnall

Supplies *Patterned paper:* Anna Griffin (light background) and Chatterbox (journaling); *Computer fonts:* Speed Bowling (title) and Jenkins (hidden journaling), downloaded from the Internet and Arial Narrow (journaling), Microsoft Word; *Stamping ink:* ColorToolBox, Clearsnap; *Pen:* Zig Millennium, EK Success; *Acrylic gel medium:* Liquitex; *Acrylic paint:* Golden Artist Colors and Plaid Enterprises; *Stencil letters:* Li'l Davis Designs; *Metal letters and corners:* Making Memories; *Fiber:* DMC.

idea to note: Create a rugged, textured border featuring a cross-hatch pattern by mixing acrylic paint with gel medium, applying a thick layer, then pressing a design into the tacky paint with a plastic knife.

SEASCAPE: by Mellette Berezoski
Supplies *Spray texture paint:* Fleck Stone, Plasti-Kote; *Sea stones, bamboo clip and starfish:* Magic Scraps; *Tags:* Making Memories; *Other:* Shells and rocks.

idea to note: Give borders a "sandy" finish with a quick spritz of texture paint. Tiny embellishments can even be pressed into the paint while it's still wet.

ADVENTURE: by Nichol Magouirk
Supplies *Patterned papers:* Pebbles Inc. and Deluxe Designs; *Embossing enamel:* Ultra Thick Embossing Enamel, Suze Weinberg for Ranger Industries; *Stamps:* Art Warehouse, Creative Imaginations; Limited Edition Rubber Stamps; *Stamping ink:* ColorToolBox, Clearsnap; *Pins:* Li'l Davis Designs.

idea to note: Stamp inked words into several layers of warm embossing enamel and remove when the enamel has cooled.

setting the tone with materials

Borders are extremely eye-catching. And the materials you choose to create them with can go a long way toward developing your page's mood and theme. Try one of these border background ideas, or experiment with a range of resources to match the feeling you're formulating:

masculine. Use metal sheets, screening, mesh, leather, wood veneer, playing cards, tiles or denim.

feminine. Incorporate lace, toile, velveteen, silk flowers, floral fabrics, watercolors, or ribbon.

childlike. Add cork, striped fabrics, vellum, diecut letters, felt, mesh, glitter, paint, blanket banding or buttons.

seasonal. Include flowers, wood veneer or embroidered papers (for spring); sea glass, sandpaper or netting (for summer); cork, raffia or burlap (for fall); and flannel, snow paste or metallics (for winter).

GONE FISHING: by Brenda Arnall

Supplies *Specialty Paper:* Sam Flax; *Stickers:* Karen Foster Design; *Acrylic paint:* Plaid Enterprises; *Mesh:* Magic Mesh, Avant Card; *Other:* Fishing swivels and jute.

idea to note: To achieve cool texture, press acrylic paint through mesh, then remove the mesh and allow it to dry before adding other embellishments.

FOLLOW YOUR BLISS: by Kelly Anderson
Supplies *Patterned paper:* Li'l Davis Designs; *Packing tape:* Manco.

how to transfer images:

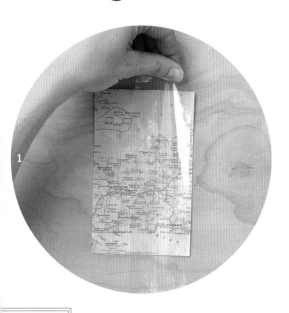

> >

> v

STEP 1: Choose an image you want to transfer and place packing tape over it. Smooth with your fingertip and then burnish with a bone folder.

STEP 2: Place in water to soak. After image has soaked for 4-5 minutes, peel the paper from the back and rub off residue under running water.

STEP 3: Once dry, the residue of glue from the tape will be sticky enough to adhere your image without using additional adhesive.

SPIRALS: by Kelly Anderson
Supplies *Chalk:* Craf-T Products; *Pen:* Zig Millennium, EK Success.

idea to note: Go for the cute, hip hand-drawn look. Create your own border with a few swirls drawn in pen, then highlight them with chalk to add even more color.

EGG HUNT: by Denise Pauley
Supplies *Patterned paper:* Arctic Frog; *Embossing template:* Lasting Impressions for Paper; *Pen:* Staedtler; *Ribbon:* Making Memories.

idea to note: After dry embossing, color your design with chalks, metallic rub-ons and more. Or, for a shabby touch, simply emboss on white-core cardstock, then lightly sandpaper your design to expose the white center.

ALL GIRL: by Mellette Berezoski

Supplies *Patterned paper, stitched tag, printed book cloth, square window, letter sticker, border strip and rivets:* Chatterbox; *Transparency:* Art Warehouse, Creative Imaginations; *Modeling compound:* Creative Paperclay Co.; *Texture stamps:* Premo, Sculpey; *Brads and acrylic paint:* Making Memories; *Other:* Cookie cutters, ribbon and floss.

idea to note: Design a pretty floral border featuring clay shapes. Apply different texture stamps to clay, cut them out with cookie cutters and paint when dry.

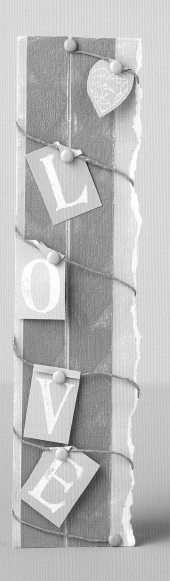

LOVE: by Miley Johnson
Supplies *Patterned paper:* Close To My Heart; *Alphabet Stamps:*
Inkadinkado (heart) and River City Stamps; *Heart stamp:* Inkadinkado;
Embossing powder: Stampin' Up!; *Brads:* Making Memories; *Other:* Twine.

 For a worn look, heat emboss on white-core card-
stock, then sand lightly to weather the paper and the embossed image.

LETTERS: by Kelly Anderson
Supplies *Ephemera:* Paper Pizazz; *Gel medium and burnt sienna glaze:*
Golden Artist Colors.

idea to note: Gel medium can be used as both an adhesive and
as a glossy coating for vintage images.

LET IT SNOW: by Denise Pauley
Supplies *Silver paper:* Emagination Crafts; *Metal mesh and tags:* Making Memories; *Snow Paste:* Delta Technical Coatings; *Alphabet stamps:* PSX Design; *Stamping ink:* StazOn, Tsukineko; *Charms:* Embellish It!, Boutique Trims; *Brads:* Magic Scraps; *Other:* Jump rings.

idea to note: Snow and texture paste can create a host of dimensional looks. Embed mesh, charms or other small items into the paste while it's still wet, or adhere later with fasteners.

FIRST CLASS: by Joy Uzarraga
Supplies *Gold leaf flakes:* Mona Lisa Products, Houston Art, Inc.; *Adhesive:* Tacky Tape, Art Accentz; Provo Craft and Scotch tape, 3M; *Vintage cutouts:* Melissa Frances.

idea to note: Use double-sided tape to adhere gold leaf flakes to your border. Vary the tape widths for added visual interest, then adhere gold leaf flakes to the top. Using a brush to carefully remove excess flakes.

ABCs: by Nichol Magouirk
Supplies *Patterned paper:* Karen Foster Design; *Paper letters:* FoofaLa; *Eyelet:* Making Memories; *Stamping ink:* Nick Bantock, Ranger Industries; *Other:* Mica and sandpaper.

idea to note: Pull mica into several layers and place them randomly over each letter. For variations in color, add additional layers over a few letters.

DRAGONFLY: by Brenda Arnall
Supplies *Specialty Paper:* Autumn Leaves; *Acrylic paint:* Golden Artist Colors; *Acrylic gel medium:* Liquitex; *Embroidery floss:* DMD, Inc.; *Other:* Fabric and charm.

how to create a textured border:

STEP 1: In a small disposable bowl, mix a spoonful of acrylic gel medium with enough acrylic paint to give you a rich color.

STEP 2: Tear off a piece of plastic kitchen wrap (like Saran Wrap) and scrunch it into a ball.

STEP 3: Dip the ball of wrap into the paint mixture.

STEP 4: Press the ball onto paper. The creases in your ball of wrap will leave ridges in the paint mixture. Repeat this process until you are happy with the design. Allow the paint to dry thoroughly then trim it down to size.

additional information

There's something to be said about "killing two birds with one stone," or in this case, having one scrapbook element serve two purposes. In addition to appearing as a decorative element, border space can also be used as an informative tool—a place to add journaling, pertinent quotes or other interesting text.

But, this doesn't mean you should simply treat the area as a long, narrow journaling box. Jazz it up with embellishments, create with color, add dimension with layers and overlays…just experiment until it's both functional and fun. Take a look at the layouts and accents in this chapter for a few ideas and insight.

BLOOM WHERE YOU'RE PLANTED: by Nichol Magouirk
Supplies *Patterned paper:* Art Warehouse, Creative Imaginations; *Epoxy words and letters:* Art Warehouse, Creative Imaginations and K & Company; *Alphabet stamps:* Hero Arts and PSX Design; *Stamping ink:* ColorToolBox, Clearsnap; *Labels:* Making Memories and Stampington & Co.; *Ribbon and eyelets:* Making Memories.

idea to note: Ground small epoxy words and letters by placing them on labels adhered to the border strip.

GIFT EXCHANGE: by Kelly Anderson
Supplies *Stickers:* Jolee's Boutique, Sticko for EK Success; *Label stickers:* Pebbles Inc.; *Twill:* Making Memories; *Alphabet stamps:* Hero Arts (large) and PSX Design (small); *Stamping ink:* Brilliance, Tsukineko; *Pen:* Zig Millennium, EK Success; *Tags:* Avery.

idea to note: Record the results of holiday gift exchanges with a clever, decorative and informative tag border.

LIFE: by Tracy Miller
Supplies *Patterned paper and sticker:* Wordsworth

idea to note: To add interest and emphasize your text, try layering a rainbow of patterned paper strips behind the words.

For Mother's Day, Daddy and the girls posed for some pictures. The girls loved on Daddy for the ca...

KISSES: by Tracy Miller
Supplies *Rub-ons:* Scrapworks; *Computer font:* Tahoma, Microsoft Word; *Other:* Ribbon.

idea to note: Colorful rub-ons adhered along the perimeter of your layout create a sense of whimsy while still conveying the message of your layout.

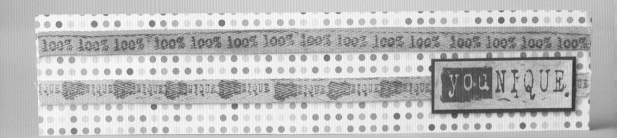

YOUnique: by Joy Uzarraga
Supplies *Patterned paper:* KI Memories; *Twill tape:* Creekbank Creations; *Stamps:* Art Warehouse, Creative Imaginations; Limited Edition Rubberstamps; *Stamping ink:* Fluid Chalk, Clearsnap (orange and pink) and Memories, Stewart Superior Corporation (brown).

how to create custom-stamped twill tape:

STEP 1: Position an ink pad (chalk or pigment inks work best) over a strip of twill tape. Pull on the end of the twill so that the ink pad runs over the length of the twill, coloring it as you pull.

STEP 2: Using a dye or solvent based ink, stamp with a border, word or letter stamps across the length of the tape.

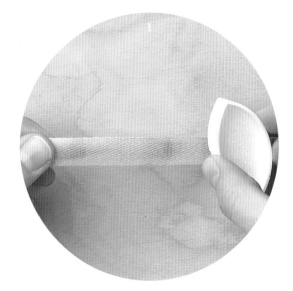

v

FUTURE'S SO BRIGHT: by Denise Pauley

Supplies *Fabric:* Junkitz; *Alphabet stamps:* Hero Arts ("loving," "loud" and "stubborn"), Making Memories ("Ryan") and PSX Design; *Stamp:* Impress Rubber Stamps; *Stamping ink:* StazOn, Tsukineko; *Rub-ons, hinges, snap and metal number:* Making Memories.

idea to note: Design a decorative border created entirely of stamped words in various sizes and styles that reflect your subject's personality.

ADVENTURE: by Jamie Waters
Supplies *Stickers:* Pebbles Inc. and Making Memories; *Other:* Ribbon, staple and paper clip.

idea to note: Snippets from definition stickers can highlight key information on collage-style borders.

IMAGINE: by Joy Uzarraga
Supplies *Patterned paper, rub-ons and tags:* Art Warehouse, Creative Imaginations; *Brads and acrylic paint:* Making Memories; *Stamping ink:* ColorToolBox, Clearsnap.

idea to note: Apply rub-ons to a row of twill tags—the result is dimensional and funky. Plus, it reflects the theme of your layout at the same time.

break up your borders

Are borders boring? Perhaps they are…relegated to the side of every layout, untouched and alone. It's sad, really. Every now and then, prevent the border blues by giving them a new shape, sizzle or style. Experiment with these concepts:

Stray from the traditional border "strip" and create one out of circles, diamonds or abstract shapes. String slide holders, charms or tags together for an eclectic look. Or, wrap fibers or ribbon around the layout's edge for a fun finish.

Bring the border onto your layout by tucking photos, dangling accents or overlapping journaling boxes onto it.

Establish a sense of motion and create a unique page dimension by positioning your border right along—or a little off—the edge. Place it on the diagonal. Turn it into a long pocket to house journaling or memorabilia. Or, tie and dangle elements from its side (compensate by trimming a little width from your background so your page will still fit inside the page protector).

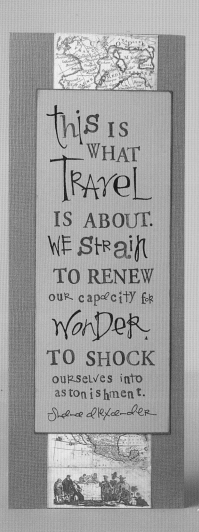

SEDONA: by Brenda Arnall
Supplies *Rub-ons:* Simply Stated, Making Memories; *Copper tag:* Nunn Design; *Copper Mesh:* Sam Flax; *Other:* Vellum and assorted brochures.

idea to note: Apply colored vellum on the top of words to soften bright colors that might conflict with pictures.

TRAVEL: by Kelly Anderson
Supplies *Patterned paper:* 7gypsies; *Rub-ons:* Making Memories; *Alphabet stamps:* PSX Design; *Stamping ink:* Brilliance, Tsukineko (black) and Stampa Rosa (brown); *Pen:* Zig Millennium, EK Success.

idea to note: An elegant quote is perfectly presented when created with a combination of stamped and handwritten letters.

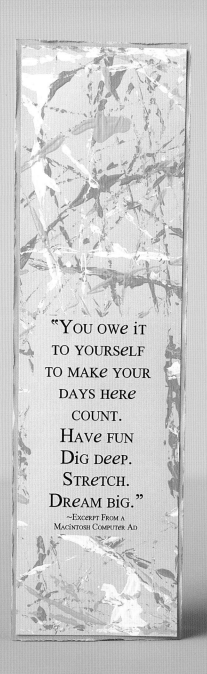

"You owe it
to yourself
to make your
days here
count.
Have fun
Dig deep.
Stretch.
Dream big."
~Excerpt From a
Macintosh Computer Ad

DREAM BIG: by Denise Pauley
Supplies *Computer font:* CK Chemistry, "Fresh Fonts" CD, *Creating Keepsakes; Acrylic paint:* Delta Technical Coatings and Plaid Enterprises.

how to paint with marbles:

STEP 1: Cover marbles liberally with acrylic paint.

STEP 2: Place cardstock inside a shallow pan. Use Post-Its to mask off any areas of the cardstock you don't want covered with paint. Place marbles on card-stock and roll back and forth until cardstock is covered with a desirable pattern. Add new paint or change colors as necessary.

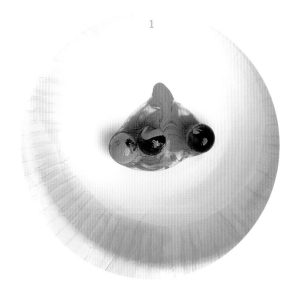

1

v

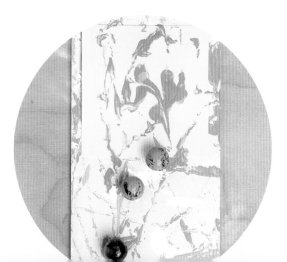

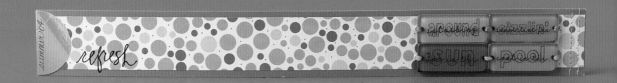

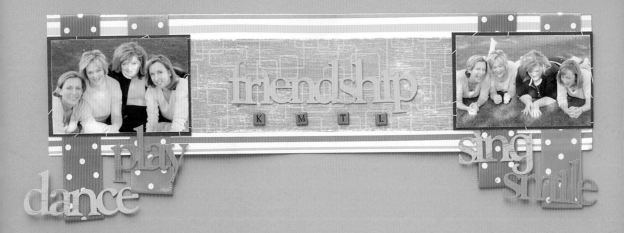

REFRESH: by Mellette Berezoski
Supplies *Patterned paper:* The Scrapbook Wizard (dotted) and Karen Foster Design (orange); *Acrylic tiles:* Junkitz; *Rub-on word and embroidery floss:* Making Memories.

idea to note: Devise a border with a message and subtle dimension using acrylic word tiles.

FRIENDSHIP: by Miley Johnson
Supplies *Patterned paper:* KI Memories; *Metal words, letters and acrylic paint:* Making Memories; *Ribbon:* C.M. Offray & Son.

idea to note: Attach words directly to ribbon to create a border with a sense of motion. Small metal letters, serving as monograms, add dimension and information.

BLOOM: by Mellette Berezoski
Supplies *Patterned paper:* The Scrapbook Wizard; *Punch-out words and accents:* KI Memories; *Rub-on word:* Art Warehouse, Creative Imaginations; *Square punch:* EK Success.

idea to note: Colorful punch-out words can form a cute, quick and easy border.

LOVE: by Joy Uzarraga
Supplies *Sticker labels and stamps:* Pebbles Inc.; *Stamping ink:* ColorToolBox, Clearsnap; *Other:* Playing cards.

idea to note: Use a Dymo label maker or label-style stickers to create a border comprised of important words.

CHRISTMAS: by Nichol Magouirk
Supplies *Woven labels:* me & my BIG ideas; *Other:* Thread.

idea to note: A collection of woven labels can convey the spirit of the season. To make the process easier, first spray a strip of cardstock with a light coat of adhesive, then affix each label before machine stitching.

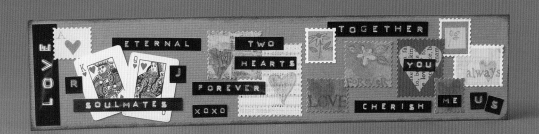

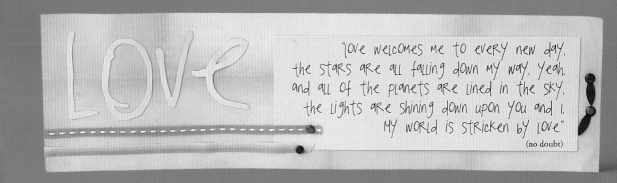

LOVE WELCOMES ME: by Jamie Waters

Supplies *Patterned paper:* Scenic Route Paper Co.; *Computer font:* 2Peas Falling Leaves, downloaded from *www.twopeasinabucket.com*, and Garamond, Microsoft Word; *Ribbon:* Making Memories; *Other:* Brads and photo turn.

idea to note: A handwritten quote mounted with ribbon and photo turns on a soft background is an effective embellishment for reflective pages.